GRAPHIC DINOSAURS

ANKYLOSAURUS

THE ARMORED DINOSAUR

ILLUSTRATED BY NICK SPENDER

PowerKiDS
press.
New York

Published in 2010 by The Rosen Publishing Group, Inc.
29 East 21st Street, New York 10010

Designed and produced by
David West Books

Designed and written by David West
Consultant: Steve Parker, Senior Scientific Fellow, Zoological Society of London
Editor: Ronne Randall
U.S. Editor: Kara Murray
Photographic credits: 5t, luc legay; 5m, goldmund100; 5b, Vall; 30 both, coolisandsong24

Library of Congress Cataloging-in-Publication Data

West, David, 1956–
Ankylosaurus : the armored dinosaur / [written by David West] ;
illustrated by Nick Spender and David West.
p. cm. — (Graphic dinosaurs)
Includes index.
ISBN 978-1-4358-8590-5 (lib. bdg.) — ISBN 978-1-4358-8596-7 (pbk.) —
ISBN 978-1-4358-8597-4 (6-pack)
1. Ankylosaurus—Juvenile literature. I. Spender, Nik, ill. II. Title.
QE862.O65W44 2010
567.915—dc22
2009015052

Manufactured in China

CONTENTS

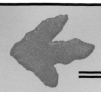
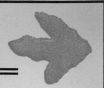

WHAT IS AN ANKYLOSAURUS?

ANKYLOSAURUS MEANS "STIFFENED LIZARD"

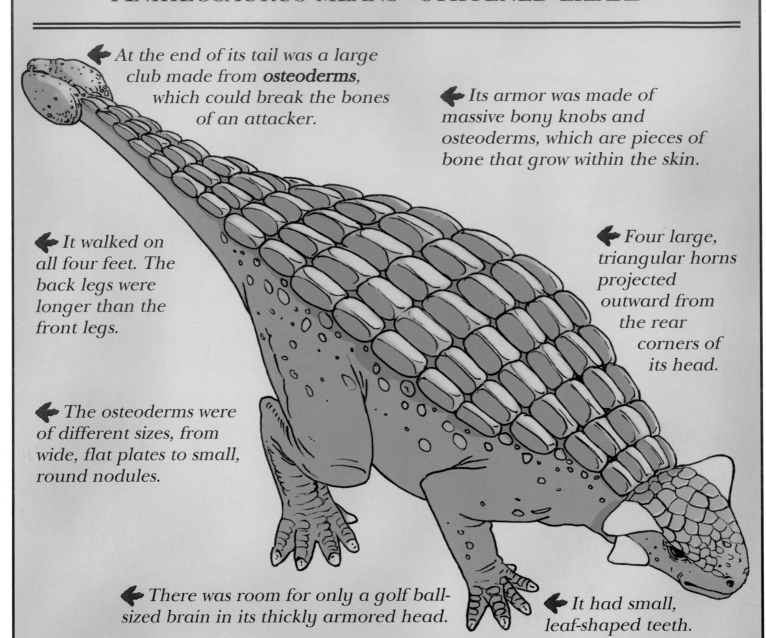

*At the end of its tail was a large club made from **osteoderms**, which could break the bones of an attacker.*

Its armor was made of massive bony knobs and osteoderms, which are pieces of bone that grow within the skin.

It walked on all four feet. The back legs were longer than the front legs.

Four large, triangular horns projected outward from the rear corners of its head.

The osteoderms were of different sizes, from wide, flat plates to small, round nodules.

There was room for only a golf ball-sized brain in its thickly armored head.

It had small, leaf-shaped teeth.

ANKYLOSAURUS LIVED AROUND 68 TO 65.5 MILLION YEARS AGO, DURING THE CRETACEOUS PERIOD. FOSSILS OF ITS SKELETON HAVE BEEN FOUND IN NORTH AMERICA (SEE PAGE 30).

Adult Ankylosauruses measured up to 25 feet (8 m) long, 6 feet (2 m) high, and 6 feet (2 m) wide. They weighed about 5 tons (4,536 kg).

A Nile crocodile

PLATE ARMOR

Ankylosaurus is one of the best-known armored dinosaurs. The bony plates were embedded in a tough, scaly skin that protected the animal from the sharp teeth of predators like Tyrannosaurus. The armored skin was similar to that of today's crocodiles.

SMALL BRAIN

Although Ankylosaurus had a small brain, it had a good sense of smell. This was useful to sniff out the flowering plants it fed on.

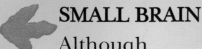

The brain was not much bigger than a golf ball.

FLOWER POWER

Ankylosauruses lived right up until the **extinction** event 65.6 million years ago, at the end of the Cretaceous period. This event was probably due to a large **meteor** or **comet** hitting our planet, causing the climate to change. Dinosaurs became extinct in a very short time. Before this, the Cretaceous period saw a huge increase in flowering plants and **pollinating** insects, such as bees. This led to an increase in the numbers and types of plant eaters, such as Ankylosaurus.

PART ONE

THE RIVER

DAY BREAKS OVER WESTERN LAURASIA (TODAY'S NORTH AMERICA). IT IS THE FINAL STAGE OF THE LATE CRETACEOUS PERIOD, AROUND 66 MILLION YEARS AGO.

YARK

YARK

YARK

ABOVE THE GRAZING ANKYLOSAURUSES, SMALL BIRDS CALLED ICHTHYORNIS FLY OUT TO THEIR FEEDING GROUNDS AT SEA.

THE BIRDS' NOISY CALLS DRAW THE ATTENTION OF A YOUNG ANKYLOSAURUS, WHO LOOKS UP.

YARK

YARK

SPLAT

IT NOTICES THAT THERE ARE TWO BRIGHT LIGHTS IN THE SKY INSTEAD OF THE USUAL ONE LIGHT.

ONE LIGHT IS A COMET CLOSE TO EARTH. ITS BODY LEAVES A TRAIL OF VAPOR THAT REFLECTS THE SUN'S LIGHT. IT WOULD POSE A THREAT TO ALL LIFE ON EARTH IF IT WERE TO COLLIDE WITH THE PLANET.

ON EARTH, THE CLIMATE IS WARM AND HUMID. THE ANKYLOSAURUSES MAKE THEIR WAY DOWN TO A RIVER. HERE THE BANKS ARE CROWDED WITH JUICY, LOW-LYING PLANTS. THEY PASS A TRICERATOPS, A PLANT-EATING DINOSAUR WITH THREE LARGE HORNS. IT IS BUSY FEEDING ON THE PLANTS WITH ITS BEAKLIKE MOUTH.

MANY OF THE PLANTS HAVE FLOWERS. BEES BUZZ FROM FLOWER TO FLOWER, HELPING POLLINATE THEM AS THEY GATHER THE NECTAR.

THE YOUNG ANKYLOSAURUS STRETCHES FOR A COLORFUL FLOWER CLOSE TO THE RIVER'S EDGE.

THE BANK BEGINS TO CRUMBLE INTO THE RIVER.

KERSPLOOSH

THE YOUNG ANKYLOSAURUS AND AN OLD BULL ANKYLOSAURUS TUMBLE INTO THE WATER.

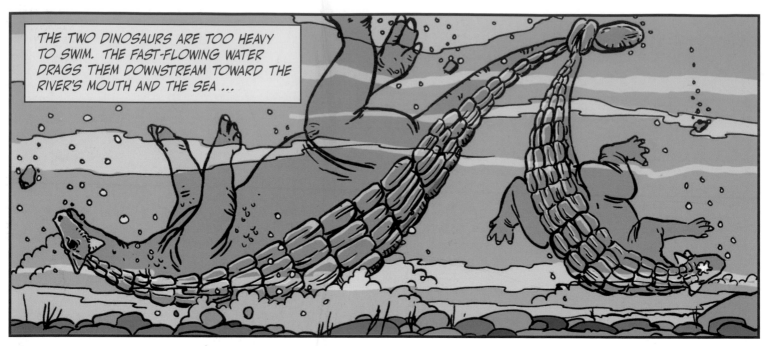

THE TWO DINOSAURS ARE TOO HEAVY TO SWIM. THE FAST-FLOWING WATER DRAGS THEM DOWNSTREAM TOWARD THE RIVER'S MOUTH AND THE SEA ...

...WHERE THEY ARE BOTH WASHED UP ONTO A LARGE GRAVEL BANK, SPLUTTERING AND COUGHING UP WATER.

COUGH

GROUGH

NONE THE WORSE FOR THE DIP, THE ANKYLOSAURUSES HEAD FOR THE BANK. NEARBY, A DARK SHAPE BREAKS THE SURFACE OF THE MUDDY ESTUARY WATER.

A GROUP OF YOUNG ORNITHOMIMUSES RACES PAST THE TWO LUMBERING ANKYLOSAURUSES. THESE SWIFT-RUNNING DINOSAURS HAVE POWERFUL REAR LEGS AND A LONG TAIL FOR BALANCE. THEY HAVE COME TO DRINK FROM THE WATER'S EDGE.

THERE IS A SUDDEN MOVEMENT AND A SPLASH. A GIANT CROCODILE CALLED DEINOSUCHUS ATTACKS ONE OF THE YOUNG ORNITHOMIMUSES.

SKREEEK

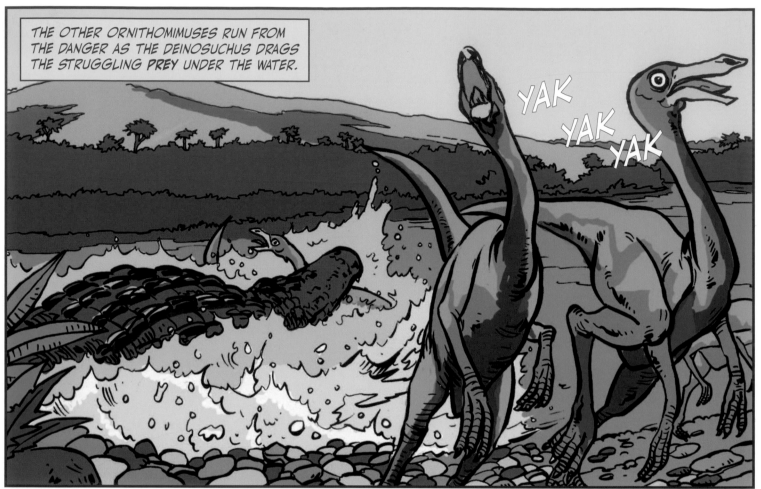

THE OTHER ORNITHOMIMUSES RUN FROM THE DANGER AS THE DEINOSUCHUS DRAGS THE STRUGGLING PREY UNDER THE WATER.

BENEATH THE SURFACE, THE GIANT CROCODILE CARRIES ITS DROWNED VICTIM TO ITS DEN UNDER THE BANK.

THE TWO ANKYLOSAURUSES ARE NOW ON THE OPPOSITE BANK FROM THE REST OF THE GROUP. THE YOUNGSTER IS UNCERTAIN WHAT TO DO.

THE YOUNG ANKYLOSAURUS IS DISTRACTED BY A BEE AS IT PASSES HIS EYES. WHERE THERE ARE BEES, THERE ARE FLOWERING PLANTS.

BZZZZZZZ

THE OLD BULL LUMBERS OFF TO A PATCH OF RICH UNDERGROWTH AND SO THE YOUNG ANKYLOSAURUS FOLLOWS WITH A GRUMBLING STOMACH.

THE TWO ANKYLOSAURUSES MOVE STEADILY AWAY FROM THE WATER. THEY CONTINUE TO MUNCH ON THE SWEET LOW-LYING PLANTS. THERE SEEM TO BE MORE BEES BUZZING AROUND THEM.

IF THEY LIFTED THEIR HEADS FOR A MOMENT, THEY WOULD SEE THE REASON WHY. ABOVE THEM, ON A TREE, IS A LARGE BEE NEST.

NEARBY IS THE ROTTING **CARCASS** OF A PARASAUROLOPHUS, A DUCK-BILLED PLANT-EATING DINOSAUR WITH A LONG BONY HEAD CREST. IT HAS BEEN HALF EATEN, AND IT STINKS.

SUDDENLY THERE IS A LOUD ROAR FROM CLOSE BY.

GWAAAAARRR!

THE GROUND SHAKES FROM THE STEPS OF A LARGE BEAST.

THE TWO ANKYLOSAURUSES STOP EATING AND LOOK UP.

ABOVE THEM A LARGE FEMALE TYRANNOSAURUS APPEARS. SHE HAS SMELLED THE CARCASS OF THE PARASAUROLOPHUS, AND SHE IS VERY HUNGRY.

BROOAARRGH

THE NEARSIGHTED OLD BULL MISTAKENLY THINKS HE IS UNDER ATTACK AND TAKES UP A DEFENSIVE POSITION. ACCIDENTALLY, HE HAS PUT HIMSELF AND THE YOUNGSTER BETWEEN THE TYRANNOSAURUS AND HER MEAL.

ROAARRR

THE YOUNG ANKYLOSAURUS HIDES BEHIND THE OLD BULL.

16

AS THE TYRANNOSAURUS STEPS AROUND THE OLD ANKYLOSAURUS, SHE NOTICES THE YOUNGSTER...

...SHE SPIES AN EASIER MEAL.

GROOAARRGH

GWEEEP

THE OLD BULL SWINGS HIS CLUB AGAIN...

...AND MISSES...

THWACK

...BUT INSTEAD HE HITS A TREE WITH A MIGHTY THWACK!

IT DISLODGES THE BEE NEST, FROM WHICH POUR HUNDREDS OF ANGRY BEES.

BZZZZZZZZZZZZZZZZZZZZZZ

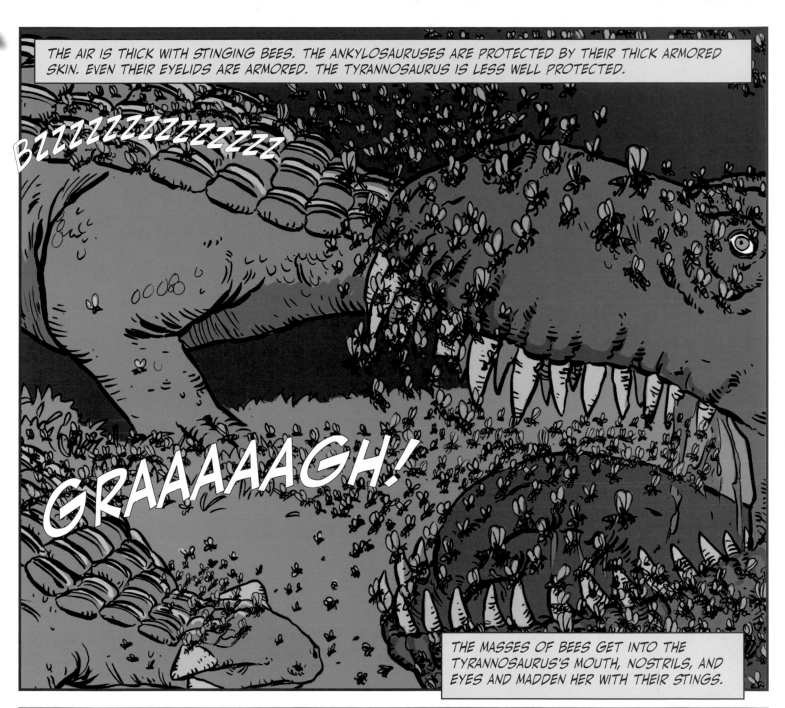

THE AIR IS THICK WITH STINGING BEES. THE ANKYLOSAURUSES ARE PROTECTED BY THEIR THICK ARMORED SKIN. EVEN THEIR EYELIDS ARE ARMORED. THE TYRANNOSAURUS IS LESS WELL PROTECTED.

BZZZZZZZZZZZZZZ

GRAAAAAGH!

THE MASSES OF BEES GET INTO THE TYRANNOSAURUS'S MOUTH, NOSTRILS, AND EYES AND MADDEN HER WITH THEIR STINGS.

THE TWO ANKYLOSAURUSES WATCH THE TYRANNOSAURUS TAKE OFF, FOLLOWED BY A CLOUD OF ANGRY BEES.

PART THREE... BIG TROUBLE

THE YOUNG ANKYLOSAURUS IS WOKEN THE NEXT MORNING BY THE SOUND OF LOUD THUMPS.

THWAP

THWAP

LEAVING THE OLD BULL SNORING IN HIS SLEEP, THE YOUNGSTER WANDERS OUT INTO AN OPEN PLAIN. HE DISCOVERS THE SOURCE OF THE SOUNDS.

THWAP

THEY ARE PACHYCEPHALOSAURUSES, STRANGE, DOME-SKULLED OMNIVORES. TWO MALES ARE BANGING THEIR HEADS AGAINST EACH OTHER'S SIDES IN A SHOW OF STRENGTH FOR THE ATTENTION OF A FEMALE.

THE YOUNGSTER STAYS CLEAR OF THE BATTLING PACHYCEPHALOSAURUSES. HE WANDERS ALONG THE EDGE OF THE FOREST AND FINDS SOME PLANTS TO FEED ON. THE LOUD THUMPS STOP.

THE PACHYCEPHALOSAURUSES SCATTER AS A GROUP OF TRICERATOPS LUMBER PAST THEM. THE TRICERATOPS HEAD TOWARD THE ANKYLOSAURUS, LOOKING FOR THE COOL SHADE OF THE TREES.

THE ANKYLOSAURUS IS WELL HIDDEN AMONG THE PLANTS, AND THE TRICERATOPS DO NOT SEE HIM.

BRRRAAAAGH

DAZED BUT UNHURT, THE YOUNGSTER HAS LANDED ON HIS BACK. HE IS IN BIG TROUBLE. HE HAS ENDED UP RIGHT NEXT TO A TYRANNOSAURUS NEST.

UP ON THE BANK OF THE HOLLOW, THE MOTHER HAS NOTICED HIM. SHE SEES THE ANKYLOSAURUS AS A DANGER TO HER EGGS.

GRRRRRRR

THE STRUGGLING ANKYLOSAURUS IS UNABLE TO ROLL ONTO HIS FEET. WITHIN A FEW SECONDS, THE TYRANNOSAURUS WILL REACH THE YOUNGSTER. HIS UNARMORED UNDERSIDE HAS NO PROTECTION AGAINST HER SHARP TEETH.

PART FOUR... THE COMET

DEEP IN SPACE, THE ICY COMET CONTINUES ON ITS PATH, NARROWLY MISSING THE PLANET EARTH. A PIECE OF THE COMET HAS BROKEN OFF AND IS BEING PULLED TOWARD EARTH BY THE PLANET'S GRAVITATIONAL FORCE.

THE PIECE IS THE SIZE OF A HOUSE. IT IS MOVING AT OVER 100,000 MILES PER HOUR (160,934 KM/H).

THE COMET PIECE HURTLES THROUGH THE EARTH'S ATMOSPHERE, LEAVING A TRAIL OF WHITE VAPOR.

WHISSSHHHHH

FIVE MILES (8 KM) ABOVE EARTH'S SURFACE, IT EXPLODES WITH ENOUGH FORCE TO BE FELT OVER 1,000 SQUARE MILES (2,590 SQ KM).

BADOOOM

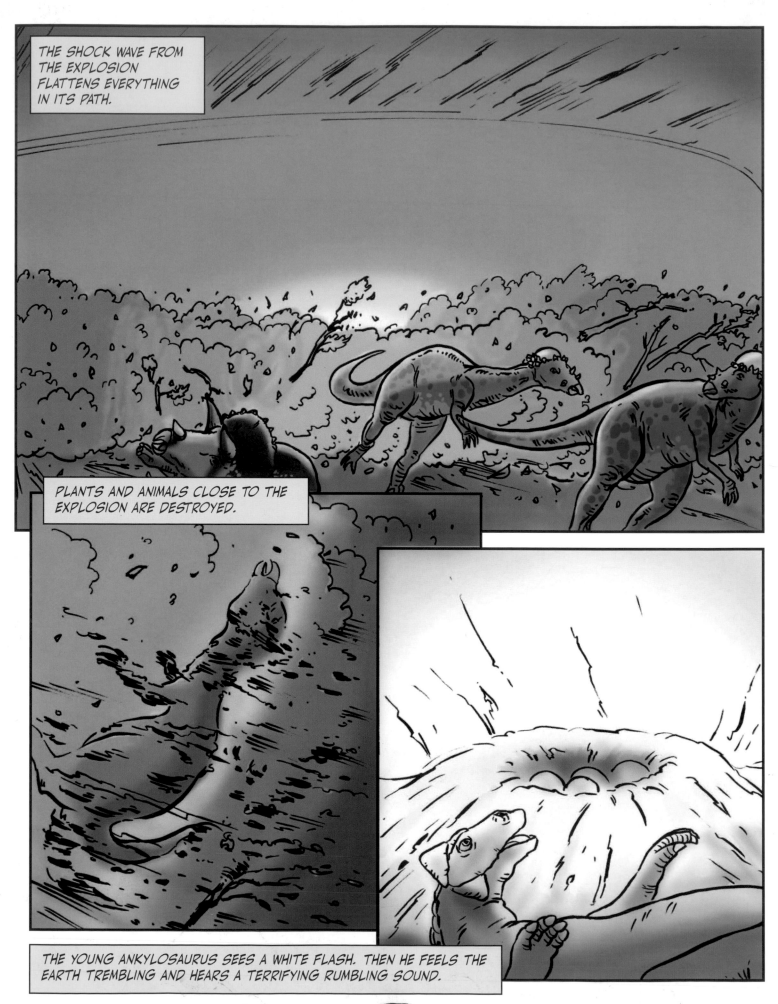

THE SHOCK WAVE FROM THE EXPLOSION FLATTENS EVERYTHING IN ITS PATH.

PLANTS AND ANIMALS CLOSE TO THE EXPLOSION ARE DESTROYED.

THE YOUNG ANKYLOSAURUS SEES A WHITE FLASH. THEN HE FEELS THE EARTH TREMBLING AND HEARS A TERRIFYING RUMBLING SOUND.

SUDDENLY THE TYRANNOSAURUS ABOVE HIM, ALONG WITH EVERYTHING ELSE, IS BLOWN AWAY IN A POWERFUL BLAST.

KRAK!

IN THE HOLLOW, THE ANKYLOSAURUS IS PROTECTED FROM THE BLAST. THE SHAKING GROUND KNOCKS THE YOUNGSTER TO HIS FEET, AND HE COWERS AS ROCKS AND STONES FALL DOWN AROUND HIM.

FINALLY THE WINDS AND THE SHAKING STOP. THE ANKYLOSAURUS HAS SURVIVED, AND HE LOOKS AROUND AT A SCENE OF DESTRUCTION.

A BEE BUZZES PAST AND THE SMELL OF SWEET PLANTS REACHES HIM. THE ANKYLOSAURUS IS HUNGRY, AND HE WALKS OFF IN SEARCH OF FOOD.

FOSSIL EVIDENCE

WE CAN GET A GOOD IDEA OF WHAT DINOSAURS MAY HAVE LOOKED LIKE FROM THEIR FOSSILS. FOSSILS ARE FORMED WHEN THE HARD PARTS OF AN ANIMAL OR PLANT ARE BURIED AND THEN TURN TO ROCK OVER MILLIONS OF YEARS.

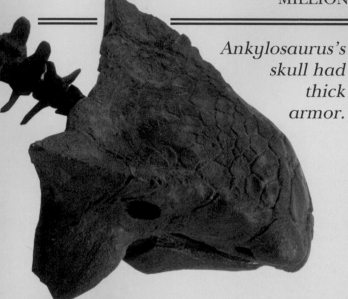

Ankylosaurus's skull had thick armor.

Fossils of Ankylosaurus have been found in rock formations dating to the very end of the Cretaceous period in western North America. Although a complete skeleton has not been discovered, several parts, such as the head, skin, and tail club, have been dug up. The famous tail club of Ankylosaurus was made of several large osteoderms, which were joined to the last few tailbones. These tailbones formed a stiff rod at the base of the club. Thick **tendons** have been preserved, which were attached to the tailbones.

These tendons were part bone and were not very elastic. This allowed a great force to be sent to the end of the tail when it was swung. It was probably a very good defensive weapon, capable of producing enough of an impact to break the bones of an attacker. It has also been suggested that the tail club acted as a pretend head to fool an attacker, although this idea is generally no longer accepted.

This fossil of an Ankylosaurus's tail club shows the large osteoderms of the club and the thick tendons of the tail.

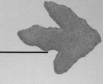

ALL THESE ANIMALS APPEAR IN THE STORY.

Ichthyornis
"Fish bird"
Wingspan: 2 ft (65cm)
A seabird with a toothed beak.

Ornithomimus
"Bird mimic"
Length: 13 ft (4 m)
A fast-running meat-eating dinosaur with a bony, toothless beak.

Pachycephalosaurus
"Thick-headed lizard"
Length: 18 ft (5.5 m)
A plant eater with a very thick and bony skull.

Parasaurolophus
"Near crested lizard"
Length: 33 ft (10 m)
A plant-eating dinosaur with a long, tube-shaped head crest and a duckbill-like mouth.

Triceratops
"Three-horned face"
Length: 26–29.5 ft (8–9 m)
A plant-eating dinosaur with a large bony frill and three horns.

Tyrannosaurus
"Tyrant lizard"
Length: 39 ft (12 m)
A huge, meat-eating dinosaur weighing over 6 tons (5,443 kg).

Deinosuchus
"Terrible crocodile"
Length: 40 ft (12 m)
A giant, extinct relative of the alligator capable of killing and eating large dinosaurs.

GLOSSARY

carcass (KAR-kus) The dead body of an animal.

comet (KAH-met) A ball of ice and dust in space that leaves a trail of gas.

Cretaceous period (krih-TAY-shus PIR-ee-ud) The period of time between 145 million and 65 million years ago.

extinction (ex-STINKT-shun) When the last member of a group of any living things has died out.

fossils (FO-sulz) The remains of living things that have turned to rock.

meteor (MEE-tee-or) A rock from space that falls to Earth.

osteoderms (OS-tee-uh-dermz) Bony parts in the skin.

pollinating (PO-luh-nayt-ing) The movement of pollen to reproduce.

prey (PRAY) Animals that are hunted for food by another animal.

tendons (TEN-dunz) The stringy parts that connect bone to muscles.

INDEX

Web Sites
Due to the changing nature of Internet links, The Rosen Publishing Group, Inc., has developed an online list of Web sites related to the subject of this book. This site is updated regularly. Please use this link to access the list:
www.powerkidslinks.com/gdino/ankylo/